IMAGES
of America

CAMP
SAN LUIS OBISPO

Maj. Gen. Walter Perry Story, the man directly responsible for the establishment of Camp San Luis Obispo, enlisted as a private during World War I. Advancing through the enlisted ranks, he was commissioned as a captain, Infantry, California National Guard (CNG), following the war. Rising to the rank of colonel and assuming command of the 160th Infantry Regiment in 1922, he inaugurated the first fully accredited officer candidate classes in the CNG. After taking command of the 40th Infantry Division, he was subsequently promoted to brigadier general in July 1926 and to major general in July 1937, assuming command of the 9th Army Corps, Fort Lewis, in 1940. He entered federal service in March 1941 and assumed command of the 40th Division, which was in training at Camp San Luis Obispo. Relieved from his command due to illness in September 1941, he retired from active service in July 1942. Having risen from the rank of private, General Story possessed an unusually deep understanding of the National Guard and its relationship to its citizen soldier.

IMAGES
of America

CAMP
SAN LUIS OBISPO

California Center for Military History

ARCADIA

George J. Albert, CPT
Mark J. Denger, CW2
Stephen S. Hedington, CW3
William W. Huss Jr., COL
John R. Justice, LTC
Brett A. Landis, WO1
Brett A. MacDonald, WO1
Roger D. McGrath, MAJ
Norman S. Marshall, LTC
Donald L. Urquidiz, LTC

ISBN 0-7385-2915-X

Published by Arcadia Publishing
Charleston SC, Chicago IL, Portsmouth NH, San Francisco CA

Printed in Great Britain

Library of Congress Catalog Card Number: 2004106567

For all general information contact Arcadia Publishing at:
Telephone 843-853-2070
Fax 843-853-0044
E-mail sales@arcadiapublishing.com
For customer service and orders:
Toll-Free 1-888-313-2665

Visit us on the internet at http://www.arcadiapublishing.com

CONTENTS

Acknowledgments   7

Introduction   9

1.   The Early Years   13

2.   Camp Merriam   31

3.   World War II   43

4.   Korean War Era   55

5.   Camp Activities and the USO   69

6.   A Period of Transformation   83

7.   Infrastructure and Revitalization   89

8.   Camp San Luis Obispo Today   99

9.   Museum and Historical Preservation   115

      California State Military Museum   128

This book is dedicated to the memory of Maj. Gen. Walter Perry Story and the men and women of the U.S. Army and California Army National Guard who have trained at Camp San Luis Obispo in the service of their state and nation.

Camp San Luis Obispo was founded in 1928 and was originally known as the National Guard Training Camp at San Luis Obispo in its early years. Later renamed in 1932 Camp Merriam, the post was renamed in honor of then Lt. Gov. (later Gov.) Frank F. Merriam. Gov. Frank F. Merriam, Maj. Gen. Walter P. Story, and his staff are pictured here at the gates of Camp Merriam.

ACKNOWLEDGMENTS

This book is the result of the collaborative efforts of the California Center for Military History, the California State Military Museum, and the Museum Annex at Camp San Luis Obispo. CW2 Mark J. Denger conceived the idea for this project and so the task of compiling this work naturally fell upon the Naval History Research & Study Element of the California Center for Military History. Directly responsible for the overall production and publication of this work, CW2 Denger worked closely with WO1 Saundra R. Peralta, Museum Annex, Camp San Luis Obispo Historical Site. Together, they deserve special recognition for graciously giving of their time and expertise to ensure the success of this project. WO1 Brett A. MacDonald and WO1 Steven Dobbins were tasked with the scanning of the hundreds of photographs required for a project of this magnitude. Maj. Roger D. McGrath, noted author and history professor, reviewed the original research material gathered by Warrant Officers Denger and Peralta and assisted in the authorship of the final draft.

An important aspect of any command is ensuring that the command functions smoothly and maintains continuity during any project. LTC Norman S. Marshall, deputy commander, accepted this challenge and has provided the inspiration and leadership responsible for the success of this work. LTC John R. Justice, operations officer, provided the necessary operational and logistics support to the Southern Area, while WO1 Brett A. Landis coordinated area personnel support. LTC Donald L. Urquidiz, CPT George J. Albert Jr., and CW3 Stephen S. Hedington provided similar support in the Northern Area. We also wish to thank the California State Military Museum and Sons of the Revolution Library for their assistance as well.

Several people from the Camp San Luis Obispo facility assisted in this work and we thank them for assisting us in this endeavor. It is clearly evident that the dedication, talent, and the commitment to duty of the members of the California Center for Military History as a whole, have resulted in this fine contribution to the military history of California. Finally, this command would also like to acknowledge Maj. Gen. Thomas Eres, Adjutant General of the State Military Forces for the State of California, Maj. Gen. John E. Bianchi, commanding general, California State Military Reserve, Brig. Gen. William G. Hamilton, commanding general, California Center for Military History, CSM Daniel Sebby, command sergeant major, California Center for Military History, Brig. Gen. (Ret.) Donald E. Mattson, chief of military history, and Lt. Col. Kelly A. Fisher, California National Guard, garrison commander, Camp San Luis Obispo, whose support made this book possible.

—William W. Huss, Jr., COL, AG, CA SMR
Commanding
Naval History Research & Study Element
California Center for Military History

Hardened guardsmen from Companies A and C, 184th Infantry, 40th Infantry Division, California National Guard, are pictured here the year just prior to the establishment of the training camp that would one day become known as Camp San Luis Obispo.

INTRODUCTION

California has a colorful military history. The central coast region, including San Luis Obispo County, has seen military activity for more than 200 years. Inhabited originally by various and occasionally warring bands of Native Americans, the first Europeans arrived when Pedro de Unamuno erected a cross and raised the imperial banner of Spain at Morro Bay in 1587. On an inland reconnaissance mission a party of his men was ambushed by local Indians, leaving two of the soldiers dead and another wounded. The Spaniards did not return until 1769 when Gaspar de Portola led a colonizing expedition into California and pioneered a coastal trail from San Diego Bay to San Francisco Bay. Portola's route came to be known to the Spaniards as El Camino Real (the King's Road), roughly Highway 101, which was the main route of travel through San Luis Obispo County.

The Spanish built Mission San Luis Obispo in 1772 and Mission San Miguel in 1797. Attached to each of these missions was a military escort, provided by the presidios at Monterey and Santa Barbara. The soldiers saw little in the way of fighting and spent most of their time assisting the mission padres in training the Indians in the skills required of Spanish settlers. In the Spanish American wars of independence that began erupting in 1808 and continued through 1821, California was mostly nothing more than an interested spectator.

When word of the successful Mexican revolution reached California in 1822, the soldiers at the Monterey presidio simply lowered the Spanish flag and raised the new Mexican banner. During the brief Mexican period, there were several mostly bloodless coups in which Mexican governors were driven from California and a local leader installed to power.

Military action of significance, though, began with the American conquest of California. From the Bear Flag Revolt and the raising of the Bear Flag, with its lone star, grizzly bear, and the words "California Republic," to the formation of the California Battalion, American military forces were soon moving from Sonoma to Monterey and then into the Salinas Valley. A sporadic, running gun battle between Col. John C. Fremont and his forces and a band of Californios occurred just north of San Luis Obispo on land that would become Camp Roberts. Fremont took possession of the Central Coast for the United States and briefly occupied Mission San Luis Obispo before moving his troops south to Los Angeles.

In September 1849, 48 delegates met at Monterey to draft a constitution for California. Among the delegates were Henry Amos Tefft and Jose Covarrubias from San Luis Obispo. Considering the monumental task facing them, the delegates completed their work quickly and had a constitution drafted by November 13, 1849. The proposed constitution was put to a vote of the people and approved at the first general election. At the same time, Peter H. Burnett was elected governor, replacing Brig. Gen. Bennett Riley, California's last military governor, on December 20, 1849.

Although not yet admitted to the Union, California had been organized and was functioning as a state. San Jose became the state's first capitol, soon followed by Vallejo, then Benicia, and, finally, Sacramento. Edward Gilbert and George Wright were popularly elected the state's first representatives to the U.S. Congress while William M. Gwin and Col. John C. Fremont were chosen by the legislature to be the first U.S. senators.

The overwhelming sentiment at the Constitutional Convention had favored immediate statehood and had rejected any consideration of territorial status. Consequently, California's congressmen-to-be lobbied for admission as a state. The California Bill, in one of the stormiest sessions of Congress on record, finally came to a vote and was approved by the Senate on August 13, 1850, and by the House on September 7, 1850. Two days later, President Millard Fillmore wrote the word "Approved" and affixed his signature under the bill signalizing the admission of California to the Union, thus adding the 31st star to the national ensign. Having bypassed the territorial stage, California became known as the Minerva State: as the mythological Minerva had burst fully developed from the head of Jupiter, California sprang into the Union without having evolved from a territory.

This would lead to the creation of California's "Militia, the army and navy of this state" as provided for in the Constitutional Convention of 1849. The last of these events—the creation of the Militia—meant that California entered the Union with an already established state military force in much the same manner, as did the original 13 colonies.

The state legislature, in the statutes of 1850, immediately provided for the formation of the California Militia. The state's militia law was patterned after the federal Militia Act of 1792. The heritage of California's "citizen soldier" dates to the American Revolution where regular or full-time forces were supplemented with reserve or part-time forces. Such a practice had its roots in the enrolled militia of Anglo-Saxon England and colonial America. The colonies depended upon the comitatus, a full-time, regular army that was backed by the limitanei or part-time soldiers charged with the defense of the state in time of emergency. While the full-time professionals were available for service anywhere, the enrolled militia was a trained and individually equipped force of citizen-soldiers who, except in times of emergency, carried on their civilian pursuits as lawyers, doctors, farmers, artisans, and merchants.

Since the state of California is nearly 750 miles in length and 250 miles in width, and has some 1,200 miles of coastline, it is greater in area than the combined states of Connecticut, Delaware, New Hampshire, New Jersey, New York, Massachusetts, Maine, Rhode Island, Ohio, and Vermont. Defense of the state—a natural concern of the people—was an almost impossible task. The 1849 Constitution conferred upon the governor the title of "commander-in-chief of the Militia," the "army and navy of this state" and conferred upon the legislature, "by law," the authority for the "organizing and disciplining the militia, in such manner as it may deem expedient, not incompatible with the Constitution and laws of the United States."

The first militia unit to be formed was actually established before the Constitution was adopted. First California Guard, Company A, 1st Regiment, Light Battery was organized in San Francisco on July 27, 1849, under the authority of Brigadier General Riley, and was later given the honor of firing the salute on the first anniversary of California's admission to the Union. The First California Guard was an artillery company but it also drilled in infantry tactics.

Acting under California Military Law, the legislature in 1852—the session was held in the then capitol city of San Jose—enacted a bill providing for the organization of a state militia. The bill divided the militia into four divisions, each commanded by a major general, and divided each division into two brigades, each commanded by a brigadier general. The governor was made commander-in-chief of the militia and he was empowered to appoint two aides-de-camp, each with the rank of colonel of cavalry. The legislature was given the authority to elect the division and brigade commanders, the adjutant general, and the quartermaster general. The latter two, like the brigade commanders, would be commissioned at the rank of brigadier general.

Several militia companies were organized from 1849 through 1862. These companies had within their ranks many men who were veterans of the Mexican War, dozens from the New York Volunteers, who had both military training and experience. Following the commencement of the Civil War, the state legislature, in 1862, reorganized the militia: staffs provided, bonds required, military duty exacted, enrollments and assessments created, muster rolls defined, the militia classified, activation of the militia determined, disciplinary procedure adopted, courts-martial established, compensation fixed, arms and equipment provided, and prior conflicting acts repealed. The number of troops raised in California during the Civil War was 16,231, more than the whole of the U.S. Army at its commencement, and far in excess of the state's quota. Altogether, 88 militia companies under various names were formed during the Civil War to serve, if required, in their respective localities, or to respond to a call from the governor.

Following the Civil War, to ensure central authority over all military units in the state, the California legislature enacted the Military Act of 1866. For the first time the state's uniformed militia force was officially designated the "National Guard of California." Moreover, the uniform for the "Guard" was to have the same appearance as that of regular U.S. Army units. In 1872, legislation formally changed the organization's name to the "California National Guard."

At the turn of the century the U.S. Army's search for a new "School of War" determined that the Edna Valley and the greater Pismo Beach area, immediately south of San Luis Obispo, were ideal locations for the school. As a result, Camp Edna was established in 1901 and Camp Pismo in 1904. Simultaneous with the latter's establishment, Gen. Arthur MacArthur organized a provisional camp to the north of San Luis Obispo on Rancho Atascadero. Regulars and guardsmen trained side by side at Atascadero during August 1904.

In 1913 federal legislation required that state militia be divided into the "organized militia" and the "reserve militia." Under the National Defense Act of 1916, the "National Guard" for the first time became an element of the U.S. Army for purposes of war. Nonetheless, the state retained the authority to train and appoint officers and the National Guard remained a part of the state's militia force, available for law enforcement and for other emergencies in the state.

Even before America's entry into World War I, the California National Guard was activated for federal service. In 1916 the Guard became part of Gen. John "Black Jack" Pershing's forces during the Mexican Border Campaign. California guardsmen soon found themselves again on active duty when the United States declared war on Germany.

Following the First World War, Congressional action provided that federal service of guardsmen should be considered as state service as well, and that all rank, privileges, exemptions, and retirement benefits gained while in federal service should apply to state service.

Although the California National Guard had served in several wars by the 1920s, the veteran outfit still had no permanent home; however, this all changed when the California legislature confirmed in the state adjutant general the power of eminent domain. Moving quickly, the adjutant general selected a site near the city of San Luis Obispo and, early in 1927, secured a 25-year lease on 2,000 acres of land. Planning for California's National Guard Training Camp, which would house up to 5,000 men, began immediately and construction was underway by the spring.

On July 4, 1928 the camp was formally opened. Still in operation today and known as Camp San Luis Obispo, the home of the California National Guard has gone through and continues to undergo many changes to meet the demands of a dynamic military force.

Today, as far as state emergency and disaster missions, the California National Guard is the most heavily tasked guard force in the United States. During the past five-years, for example, over 50 percent of this nation's emergency response call-ups were performed by the California National Guard. During times of earthquakes, civil disturbance, floods, wildfires, and search and rescue, the California National Guard is always ready, always there, ensuring the safety and security of the citizens of our state. But the California National Guard's primary reason for being is its federal mission. And, in order to maintain optimum readiness in the event of mobilization, it engages in numerous military training exercises at home and abroad.

From their humble beginnings in 1849, the state's military forces, now including the adjutant general, California Army National Guard and California Air National Guard, California State Military Reserve, California Cadet Corps, and California Naval Militia, have grown and evolved and have each played a vital role in the defense and security of this state and the nation. The story of Camp San Luis Obispo, the original home for these forces, is as much their story as it is our history. This story is told here through a series of historic photographs selected from the collections of the camp and from the California State Military Museum. The photographs capture the development of the camp from its establishment in 1928 to its modern configuration in the 21st century and many of the men and women who have served their state and nation as citizen soldiers through war and peace.

One

THE EARLY YEARS

Camp San Luis Obispo has been officially designated the original home of the California National Guard. From 1850 through 1927, units of the California Militia, later known as the California National Guard, were forced to conduct their summer training on private ranches, in state parks and, to a limited extent, on federal military installations in the state. In the years following World War I the need for a state-owned training site became widely recognized. Temporary training camps were established at Edna, Pismo, and Nacimiento in 1901, and at Atascadero in 1904. The Guard trained at Camp Atascadero in 1904, 1908, 1910, and 1912. During the other years of the early 20th century training was conducted at Edna, Pismo, or Nacimiento or at Camp Del Monte, near Monterey, one of the federal government's "Citizen Military Training Camps." As the California National Guard's strength grew from 3,200 to 5,600 men even the spacious Del Monte training site was stretched to its limits.

Brig. Gen. Richard E. Mittelstaedt, state adjutant general, and Brig. Gen. Walter P. Story, commanding general of the 40th Infantry Division, together with State Senator Chris N. Jesperson and Assemblyman Frank Merriam, persuaded the state legislature that a permanent post was needed for the California National Guard. Various locations were considered before a site was chosen near San Luis Obispo, ideally situated halfway between California's two major population centers. In early 1927, a 25-year lease was secured for 2,000 acres of ranch land along Highway 1, just west of San Luis Obispo. Planning began immediately for what was designated National Guard Training Camp, San Luis Obispo, and construction of camp facilities, including housing for up to 5,000 men, was underway by summer.

By the spring of 1928 Regimental Area No. 2 was completed, with all necessary warehouses and corrals. As a direct result of the combined efforts of Generals Mittelstaedt and Story and legislators Jesperson and Merriam, the National Guard Training Center was officially opened on July 4, 1928. During the next several months Regimental Area No. 1, a swimming pool, a PX, an officers club, and a headquarters and other administrative units were built. Cost of construction was some $500,000.

In the statutes of 1928, the California legislature confirmed in the state Adjutant General the power of eminent domain. As a consequence, on July 1, 1929, the state purchased the 2,000 acres of land that it had been leasing for $163,000. Known then as the Jack Ranch, the land was originally a part of the old Rancho El Chorro land grant.

The camp derived its name from Mission San Luis Obispo de Tolosa, founded by Fr. Junipero Serra in 1772 as the fifth of 21 missions in the California chain, and named after Saint Louis of Toulouse, the son of the king of Naples and a 13th century bishop. The scenic San Luis Obispo region, with the mission and its thriving cattle ranches, still reflects the historic influences of Spain and Mexico.

In its early years Camp San Luis Obispo was called the National Guard Training Camp, San Luis Obispo. The camp primarily served as the summer home to the 40th Infantry Division.

14

Nestled in the beautiful Chorro Valley at the foot of the Santa Lucia Mountains of the Pacific Coast Range, the camp lies midway between Los Angeles and San Francisco, and a short distance from Morro Bay. Before the Stars and Stripes were unfurled over the area those of three other nations were raised-Spain, Mexico, and California Republic.

The road sign in this photograph points the way to the entrance to the National Guard Training Camp.

Even before the modern-day scenic Pacific Coast Highway (State Route 1) was built through the area, the Headquarters building, seen here, and the officers club were erected at the National Guard Training Camp, San Luis Obispo.

The first encampment took place at Camp San Luis Obispo in 1929. Pictured here astride his horse, Brig. Gen. Walter P. Story had used his influence to persuade state officials of the need to establish the National Guard Training Camp at San Luis Obispo.

General Story inspects the troops on the camp's parade ground, located a short distance from the headquarters building. For the first time National Guard commanders from the northern and southern parts of the state could effectively train all of the troops at one location.

On a hill just above the headquarters building was the infantry camp where guardsmen, such as those of Company I, 159th Infantry pictured here, became proficient in setting up camp.

The National Guard Training Camp became an important placing for drilling. Company H, 160th Infantry Regiment is seen here drilling on the parade ground. The infantry camp can be seen off in the distance.

Company C, 3rd Battalion, of the 185th Infantry, prepare for inspection.

While the life of an infantryman in camp was hard, it did have its enjoyable moments. The pup tent not only served as shelter but a place of retreat at the day's end.

The self-sacrifice and patriotism of a freedom-loving people can be seen in this guardsman. Armed with a Model 1917 Enfield rifle and wearing a campaign hat and puttees (canvas leggings), he is prepared to fight in times of emergency. As the embodiment of the state, the citizen-soldier carries on the nation's fine and worthy militia traditions, dating to early colonial America.

An infantryman traveled light. While training in the field, two men were assigned to a tent and during an inspection, as pictured here; their gear was carefully arranged for display.

Field medics stand alongside their ambulance. Often treating sunburns and snakebites, they were trained and ready to administer emergency care for serious wounds and injuries. In the background are some of the camp's horses, which played a prominent role as a part of artillery and infantry maneuvers. Well into the 1930s guardsmen were trained in cavalry tactics as well as infantry.

The field communications center is an important aspect of National Guard training. Here members of the Signal Corps are trained using the wireless telegraph, signal flags, and various other forms of communications such as the heliograph.

World War I radically changed the face of infantry warfare. Following the conflict, the U.S. Army trained extensively with a new instrument of war—the tank. Pictured is a World War I, French-designed Renault FT-17 armed with a dummy cannon and used for training.

One of the highlights of the soldiers' day was "chow time." Each company had its own mess wagon or field kitchen and the men regarded the unit cooks favorably.

The field kitchen and the camp cooks have always been an important part of Army life. Posing for the camera are cooks from Company C, 185th Regiment. Chow wagons served each company. Eventually, these chow wagons would be replaced with company dining facilities.

While training in the field, soldiers would line up with their mess tins to receive their rations from the unit cooks. Standing patiently in the chow line at a mess wagon are infantrymen from the 160th Regiment.

During the summer months the morning fog was frequently thick, making for cool temperatures, while the afternoon brought clear skies and temperatures reaching into the high 80s. As can be seen from the faces of these soldiers, chow time was always a welcome break from training in the summer sun.

During its early years Camp San Luis Obispo was used as a reserve training area for both mounted and dismounted training. In practical terms, an artillery commander had greater responsibility than did a commander of infantry. While both commanders had to care for about 100 men, seeing to their training, arming, clothing and equipping, feeding, and discipline, the artillery commander had the added responsibility to care for 100 horses, supervising their equipping, training, feeding, and grooming.

A lieutenant for each section, consisting of two guns, accompanying men, horses, limbers, and caissons, assisted the artillery captain. Each gun detachment was under the command of a sergeant, "the chief of the piece." When in action, each gun, with one limber supplying ammunition, was commanded by a gunner, usually a corporal, and the caisson, with an additional limber, was stationed to the rear under command of another corporal. Drivers, who handled the horses, and cannoneers, who manned the guns, were privates.

Horse-drawn field artillery units were used well into the 1930s. The artillery commander was responsible for 6 field pieces, 14 to 20 limbers, 6 caissons, a traveling forge, a battery wagon, and 2 supply wagons. The 143rd Field Artillery Regiment, pictured here, was assigned to infantry support. Although termed "mounted artillery," the cannoneers marched on foot.

During these early years, the hills and valleys of the National Guard Training Camp, San Luis Obispo, were ideally suited for field training as even the infantry had to endure mounted training as seen here with the 160th Infantry Regiment.

Soldiers from the 159th Infantry gather feed for their unit's mounts. Guardsmen quickly learned that the joys of mounted training came with many additional duties and responsibilities.

Soldiers from Company A, 184th Infantry, water down their mounts after a long ride.

Lieutenants Persinger and Philpott of the 185th Infantry are pictured on their mounts in the hills above the camp.

Two

CAMP MERRIAM

The first official encampment at National Guard Training Camp, San Luis Obispo took place in 1929. At this and subsequent encampments the troops were quartered in what amounted to tent cities, located at the fringes of the newly constructed Main Garrison. As a result of the stock market crash during the fall of 1929 and the onset of the Great Depression, the early years of the 1930s saw the California National Guard struggle to maintain its peacetime requirements of weekly drills and annual summer encampments at San Luis Obispo. Nevertheless, the National Guard Training Center continued to increase in size and not all the funding for new construction came from government sources. Calling upon the patriotic spirit of the California citizen-soldier, guardsmen were asked to subscribe to the camp's Recreation Fund and to make regular contributions. Responding as generously as circumstances would allow, guardsmen contributed enough money to build much needed recreational facilities at the camp.

By 1932 the National Guard Training Camp had grown to 5,800 acres and had acquired a new name, Camp Merriam. Named for then Lt. Gov. (later Gov.) Frank F. Merriam, the camp owned its very existence to the Iowa-born Republican who fought vigorously for the National Guard and the camp while speaker of the state assembly, then presiding officer of the state senate, and later lieutenant governor.

Lying halfway between Los Angeles and San Francisco on a major highway, the National Guard Training Center was conveniently located for guardsmen from California's two principal cities. Additionally, San Luis Obispo County had rail links with both Los Angeles and San Francisco, a sizable seaport, the city of San Luis Obispo with all its services, and rugged terrain for training troops.

When war erupted in Asia and then in Europe during the late 1930s, military activity at Camp Merriam increased sharply. Along with the increase came a division of the facility into the artillery camp and the larger infantry camp. During April 1937 the first of many troop trains arrived at San Luis Obispo. Loaded with supplies and packed with soldiers for training at Camp Merriam, the train signaled the start of a buildup that would accelerate dramatically during 1940 and 1941 under the U.S. Army.

Yet in 1937 when that first troop train arrived, the residents of San Luis Obispo were only vaguely aware of mounting hostilities with Japan and the military's increased interest in the training facility at Camp Merriam.

Pictured from left to right, Maj. Gen. Walter P. Story, Gov. Frank F. Merriam, and Brig. Gen. Harry Moorhead stand in front of the camp's main gate, built in 1928 using local river rock.

The National Guard Training Camp, San Luis Obispo, proved to be an ideal summer training ground for the California National Guard. In 1932 the camp was renamed Camp Merriam, in honor of Lt. Gov. Frank F. Merriam, a longtime supporter of the California National Guard. As a member of the state legislature, Merriam had been instrumental in establishing the original camp. He would become governor of California in 1934 upon the death of Gov. James Rolph Jr.

Prior to 1932, only a small cluster of administrative buildings marked Camp Merriam. The first buildings constructed on the camp, the headquarters building and officers' club, were built in 1928. Other buildings, including a caretaker's house, barns, and corals had been completed in 1929. But most of the post's housing consisted of tents and very little additional construction was really needed on the post until 1934.

Colonel Blood relaxes at the company headquarters in the mid-1930s. By this time the camp had been divided into separate encampment areas, allowing for independent artillery practice and infantry training.

The officers' mess is pictured here during summer training in 1934. Unlike the early days, the field kitchen of the mid-1930s was mounted on a vehicle. Without modern refrigeration, the field kitchen relied on an icebox. Even as technology advanced, the preferred drinks in the field were coffee, iced tea, or water.

This soldier demonstrates the art of camouflage.

Battalion supply officers relax in one of the early sheet metal buildings constructed near the camp's motor pool.

No Army can operate without senior NCOs tending to a myriad of details. A sergeant first class from the 160th Infantry Regiment prepares essential reports for Headquarters.

Both the Browning water-cooled .30 caliber machine gun, pictured here, and the .50 caliber were used by American soldiers during both World Wars.

Soldiers of Company A, 160th Infantry, practice with a 37 mm field piece. This short-range weapon dates to World War I and was still in use as late as 1942. The 37 mm field cannon could be easily disassembled for mobility and used when field artillery support was unavailable.

The Browning .30 caliber machine gun was also an effective anti-aircraft weapon, making it a very versatile tool for ground troops.

A crew of five services this 75 mm Howitzer.

A crew of seven from the 143rd Field Artillery Regiment services a 155 mm Howitzer. One of the larger cannons in the National Guard arsenal, because of its size, the 155 mm Howitzer had to be towed by motor truck.

Guardsmen from the 143rd Field Artillery Regiment fire an American built 75 mm field gun, patterned after a French design, which formed part of a three-gun battery assigned to support the infantry field positions. Capable of firing 10 rounds every minute, these 75 mm field guns prior to the late 1920s had wooden spoke wheels, which were converted to rubber in the mid-1930s.

From a position well above the action, officers and staff from the 143rd Field Artillery Regiment observe both spotters, with their optical range finders, and field artillery positions while guardsmen using field telephones communicated corrections to the gun crews.

The 40th Infantry Division is pictured here on the parade ground. Captain Wunderlick of Company I, Captain Love of Company K, and Captain Pettit follow Lieutenant Heckert and Major Winans, Headquarters Company, as they lead the 3rd Battalion, 185th Infantry Regiment.

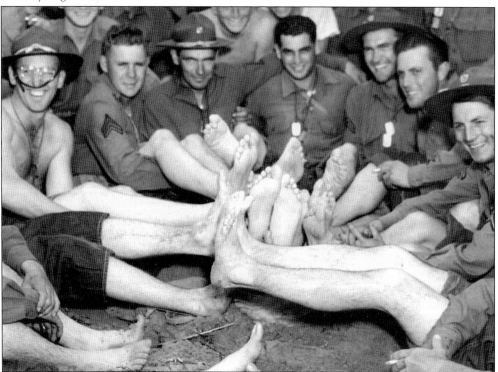

Guardsmen from the 159th Infantry Regiment clearly show the effects of a typical 20-mile march on the feet.

Pictured here is a typical summer bivouac at Camp Merriam during the 1930s.

An experienced soldier will always manage to stay clean, washed, and warm even in the field.

Col. Ray W. Hays, commanding officer, 185th Infantry Regiment, takes a moment to relax outside his tent during a period of intensive training.

Field engineers from the 184th Infantry take the machine shop directly into the field. While one vehicle contained lathes, grinders, and drill presses, the other was a mobile warehouse of frequently used parts.

Three

WORLD WAR II

When France fell in the summer of 1940, a general mobilization of the California National Guard saw troops move from their armories to their old training grounds at Camp Merriam. Shortly thereafter, the federal government exercised its preemptive rights and leased Merriam from the State of California, renaming the National Guard's facility Camp San Luis Obispo. Mobilized on March 3, 1941, California's 40th Infantry Division, under the command of Maj. Gen. Walter P. Story, was ordered to the camp. Also arriving at the camp were guardsmen from Arizona, Nevada, and Utah. Ultimately, several infantry divisions would train at the camp before begin deployed overseas during World War II.

To accommodate the thousands of troops arriving weekly, the camp was enlarged by 4,685 acres early in 1941. Title to this acreage was vested in the Department of the Army. At the same time the Army also acquired 4,170 acres at the headwaters of the Salinas River, about 20 miles east of Camp San Luis Obispo. Total area available to the Army for training now amounted to more than 14,000 acres of both federal and state land. Construction also attempted to keep pace with the increase in numbers of troops. However, during the winter of 1941 heavy rains, up to 36 inches from January through March, slowed construction to a crawl. Lacking proper drainage, the camp became a swamp while building costs rose by $17 million. Harry S. Truman, a junior senator from Missouri, would make a name for himself by investigating the "enormous cost overruns" associated with the construction at Camp San Luis Obispo.

By summer 1941, the camp's main cantonment area was completed and the 14,000-acre training facility blossomed into one of the largest and busiest in the nation. Within 48 hours of Japan's sneak attack on Pearl Harbor, though, Camp San Luis Obispo became a virtual ghost town. Expecting a Japanese invasion of the West Coast, elements of the 40th Infantry Division were moved to defensive positions over a 350,000-square-mile area that stretched from Southern and Central California to Yuma, Arizona, and Salt Lake City, Utah. From 1940 through 1945, Camp San Luis Obispo hosted a total of some 500,000 troops, although no more than 10,000 would be based there at any one time. In addition to training American soldiers, Camp San Luis Obispo also served as an internment compound for Italian and German prisoners of war (POWs). After the surrender of Italy in 1943, many of the Italian POWs remained at the camp and joined the U.S. Army Service Units.

Camp Merriam was deactivated as a National Guard training facility when the federal government assumed command of the post in 1940. The work of expanding the camp had already begun when Col. Henry T. Bull assumed command of Camp San Luis Obispo in December 1940 while some 7,000 workmen were still on the job of construction. At that time the camp's name was officially changed from Camp Merriam to its present name Camp San Luis Obispo.

During the winter of 1940–1941 construction of the main cantonment area was hampered and began to drive the costs spiraling upward when 36 inches of rain fell in the San Luis Obispo area. Even though construction of Camp San Luis Obispo was commenced in the fall of 1940,

The camp was first a city of pyramidal tents among miles of roads and streets, parade grounds, ranges, and basic utility installations. By the time the work was finished in 1941, California's 40th Division already completed its training. Other Army divisions including the 6th, 7th, 35th, 81st, 96th, 97th, and 104th, began arriving to receive training here during this same timeframe.

it would not be completed until early summer of 1941 at a cost of more than $17 million—an inordinate amount of money in 1941.

Thousands of loaves of bread were baked daily at the central bakery for later distribution among the company messes.

Two baker's dozen, and then some, kept the ovens going around the clock and made countless breadstuffs and pastries.

Beef was an important staple to the American GI diet since a high-protein diet was essential for strength. Most of the beef used was purchased from local ranchers and farmers.

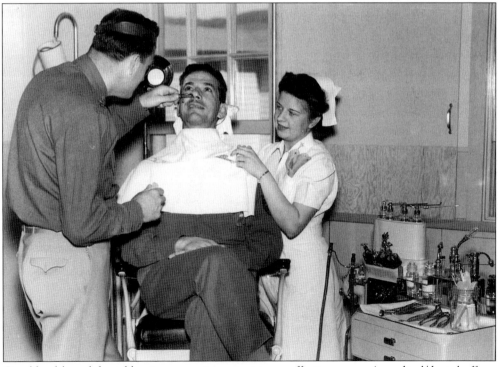

Good health and dental hygiene were important to an effective army. A medical/dental officer and assistant examine a soldier from the 40th Infantry Division.

The mailroom was a crucial part of military morale and necessary for business communication.

The logistics required to keep Camp San Luis Obispo operating smoothly through the war years required a lot of materials and supplies. Here men from the Quartermasters Corps off-load supplies from the special train siding that had been built in the late 1930s. Note the chains on the front tires that were required due to the mud left by the rains of 1941.

Good-running equipment was as important as a healthy soldier. This mobile machine and repair shop, c. 1941, kept equipment running both on post and in the training field.

Highly trained military and civilian personnel who kept and processed records in good order staffed Camp San Luis Obispo's headquarters and administrative buildings.

Much of the instruction came from highly trained "old timers" versed in the art of soldiering. Recruits, like this lad, had much to learn and this sergeant shares his valuable training with the 1917 Model Enfield rifle.

Transportation of troops from one place to the next was an import part of Army's logistics. The "deuce and a half" served as the backbone of the Army's transportation vehicle. Here we see a column of these trucks built by GMC led by a command scout vehicle.

Tens of thousands of infantry soldiers would eventually receive their training here. Here the 160th Regiment, Headquarters Company, arrives at the camp.

The DUWKS (amphibious trucks) were introduced to the Army in 1942 and were used by the troops in practice on makeshift beachheads at Morro Bay.

Members from the 222nd Field Artillery Regiment take time to pose for this photograph during 1941 maneuvers.

Members from Company A, 159th Infantry Regiment, 40th Division, pause for this photograph upon tear-down of their tents in preparation for their final departure from Camp San Luis Obispo.

Deploying overseas, members of Company H, 160th Infantry Regiment, 40th Division, pause for this photograph.

With the 40th Division departing from Camp San Luis Obispo, this Tin Lizzie (1927 Model "T") shows the optimism of the troops for an early return home. The note on the side door reads: "Please keep air in the tires at 35 lbs."

Four

KOREAN WAR ERA

As requested by Brig. Gen. Curtis D. O'Sullivan, adjutant general of California, the U.S. Army relinquished its pre-emptive rights and returned Camp San Luis Obispo to the State of California and the National Guard in 1946. The cantonment area not previously owned by the state, including all improvements on both sides of the highway, was ceded to California in lieu of restoration. During this time Camp San Luis Obispo became home to the United States Property and Fiscal Office for California (USPFO). The USPFO continues to provide logistical and fiscal support for the California National Guard.

Concurrent with the return of the camp to the state was the reorganization of the California National Guard. When the National Guard was reconstituted after World War II, it was determined that the state could support two infantry divisions: the newly organized 49th Infantry Division, consisting of the 159th, 184th and 185th Infantry Regiments, and the 40th Infantry Division, consisting of the 160th Infantry Regiment and the newly organized 223rd and 224th Infantry Regiments. For a number of years, the camp served as the training site for both the 40th and 49th Infantry Divisions as well as for several non-divisional elements.

For a brief period, the California National Guard settled into a routine of scheduled drills and annual training at Camp San Luis Obispo. Then, on June 25, 1950, the North Korean People's Army invaded the Republic of Korea. Two days later, the United States was again at war. Within a month Camp San Luis Obispo was activated by the U.S. Department of Defense for the Korean Conflict. Following suit, the U.S. Army mobilized the 40th Infantry Division and other elements of the Guard at Camp San Luis Obispo.

From December 1951 to October 1953 the camp became home to the Southwestern Signal Corps Training Center. Included in the command was the Southwestern Signal Replacement Training Center, which put 12,862 recruits through basic training and trained another 8,642 signal corps technicians. Another advanced school at Camp San Luis Obispo was the Southwest Signal School. The Southwest Signal School graduated 5,415 signal corps specialists. The 505th Signal Group, consisting of 5 Signal Battalions also trained at the camp from January 1952 to September 1953.

Thousands of new recruits were processed through the new Southwestern Signal Corps Training Center at Camp San Luis Obispo. The mission of the Southwestern Signal Corps Training Center was to provide the specific training for Signal Corps personnel including basic military training and certain technical courses. Other courses including pole line construction, teletypewriter, and telephone switchboard operation, signal message clerk, and telephone installer and repairman classes were conducted by the Basic Training and Technical Training Groups of the Southwestern Signal Replacement Training Center. Specialized unit training for the various Signal Corps organizations fell under the direction of the 505th Signal Corps.

Before students began their course of instruction they were required to draw the necessary field equipment from the field training supply center.

Incoming recruits were first greeted and received their basic orientation from Brig. Gen. Harry Reichelderfer, commanding general, Southwestern Signal Corps Training Center, Col. Marlin S. Moody, commanding officer, Southwestern Signal Replacement Training Center, and Lt. Col. James A. McClung, commanding officer, Basic Training Group, and were constantly reminded by a sign posted at head of chow line at the corps main command post of the prices of all equipment issued to them.

Every student was issued a carbine. The weapon's serial number was recorded and the student was responsible for the weapon issued him or her throughout the training.

Prior to their first march into the field, students roll their packs at the field training supply center.

Receiving instruction on pack rolling at the supply point was an important phase of their training as the proper distribution of weight was essential. After completing instruction in pack rolling students were loaded on to vehicles to be transported to the basic orientation classroom where they received additional training.

Pictured here is the field training orientation at Theater #1.

Students attend orientation at corps main command post run by the day officer in charge, or OIC, to learn about their respective jobs out in the field.

The OIC at the 402nd Signal Battalion's division headquarters is seen here giving orientation to students. In addition to the Basic Training Group and Technical Training Group, the Replacement Training Center also operated the Leaders' Course, which trained outstanding soldiers for future assignments as leaders of Signal units. These students were usually the OIC instructor to the students attached to the Technical Training Group.

Here soldiers learn how to put up the command post tent at the 402nd Signal Battalion's division advance position. With teamwork, the command post tent at the 402nd Signal Battalion's division's advance position goes up quickly and soon the communications equipment is brought in and will be operating as the division's command post or headquarters.

After receiving basic orientation, it was now out to the field. Most often, the troops had to march to the next training area.

Here a student sets up the PE-75 portable generator that will provide the necessary electricity needed at the 401st Signal Battalion's division advance command post.

Here a soldier receives instruction as to how to install field wire lines near the 401st Signal Battalion's division command post.

MEANS CHART

UNIT	RAD	TT	TP
COM CORP	NONE		
02 ARMY	NONE		

Students and instructors are pictured here manning the communications center at the 402nd Signal Battalion's advance command post.

Students were required to put into practice the art of actually operating a switchboard and I&M mainframe in the field at the 402nd Signal Battalion division headquarters advance position in order to escalate to the next phase of their training.

While students were being trained in the classroom, others were in the field, and still others learned first hand by operating the TC-10 switchboard at Camp San Luis Obispo's army headquarters.

Students had to learn how to dig holes and place telephone poles for their installation.

Pole Orchard was used primarily to teach students how to repair telephone lines before actually having to try it on the pole. There were actually three or four different types of pole orchards

Pole work required students to install a lead covered cable line from pole to pole. Here we see the pole work almost finished as the students complete the installation of the lead covered cable line from headquarters to the corps main command post.

for use in teaching specific courses.

Students operate carrier equipment at the corps main command post.

Orientation training was then conducted in a classroom in the field.

Students were given more instruction in another field classroom.

The course instruction was intense. Soldiers were required to continue their education in weapons training as well as technical training.

Here students are back on the range in order to keep up their weapons proficiency before being deployed overseas.

Five

CAMP ACTIVITIES
AND THE USO

The United Service Organizations (USO) began in 1941 as Hollywood and the nation rallied to support the war effort. The story of the USO's first half-century parallels much of the history of Camp San Luis Obispo. For over 50 years the USO has represented the best of Hollywood and the American people—compassion, magnanimity, selflessness, and service. Wherever our soldiers have gone, so to has the USO. And with them scores of celebrities, entertainers, professional ballplayers, Miss America, and of course Bob Hope.

Bringing entertainment to our troops, stateside and abroad, the USO show of World War II conjures up the image of the comedian and musicians on a makeshift stage surrounded by thousands of troops and a singer belting out the saga of the "Boogie Woogie Bugle Boy of Company B." But the USO was far more than just a military show. The USO also operated some 3,000 USO service centers, canteens, and clubs nationwide.

In addition to the NCO and officers' clubs on post, USO centers were intended to provide armed forces personnel with a "home away from home," a place where a soldier could spend time outside the strict military atmosphere. Young women from the local community volunteered as hostesses, providing civilian contact at dances, parties, and other social activities. In addition to providing camp shows, the USO also provided other services through its USO Star Spangled Network, such as a portable recording studio where a soldier could record a message and send it back home. The USO came to an end in on January 9, 1948, having fulfilled its original purpose.

Three years later, with the conflict in Korea, followed by the Vietnam War, the USO was back in action again. Unlike the USO in World War II, which had concentrated most of its support services stateside, USO centers were established outside the United States. Still, the soldiers of Camp San Luis Obispo saw their share of Hollywood stars pass through its gates throughout World War II, the Korean War, and even the Vietnam era.

To the USO and the hundreds of performers who have unselfishly given their time and talents to entertain our military forces, to the volunteers serving coffee and sandwiches here at home, and to those individuals of San Luis Obispo who generously supported the USO organization, California's military forces thank you for the memories.

Social functions have always been an important part of military life, and the officers' club remains an important center for social events. Very little has changed since the officers' club was built in 1928.

This interior view of the officers' club shows why it is still a popular location for holding wedding receptions and other social events.

Little has changed since the non-commissioned officers' club was constructed in 1941. Like the officers' club, the NCO club is primarily utilized for social events conducted by transitory units training at Camp San Luis Obispo.

This picture provides an interior view of the NCO club today.

Camp San Luis Obispo's gym has been utilized for many types of events. Boxing competitions were not only popular among the units, but also served to instill a sense of spirit during World War II and the Korean War eras.

Sports have always been an important part of military life. Team sports like football, baseball, basketball, and volleyball not only instilled pride in company teams, it also served as a favorite form of recreation during the war years.

Sports are an important part of army life. The rivalry between units made sporting events like this basketball game very popular events.

Here sporting gear is being distributed to units. While team sports instilled a sense of pride, individual sports were also encouraged as a means of fitness training.

In times of war and in times of peace, social events, such as this dance held during World War II, are an integral component of military life.

Another important part of military life centers on music. Army bands and orchestras provided troops with entertainment and inspiration. Music stirs the soul and can help instill the patriotic spirit needed by the fighting man.

Young women from the local community volunteered as hostesses, providing civilian contact at dances, parties, and other social activities.

This World War II photograph depicts the 40th Infantry Division band at Camp San Luis Obispo in the early years of the war.

Troops line up to watch a wartime movie at War Department Theater. Today this theater is known as the PerLee Theater named after Brig. Gen. Theron R. PerLee, the first adjutant general of California (April 1850–October 1850).

The camp's amphitheater was a very popular site as many of Hollywood's greats such as Bob Hope, Dorothy Lamour, and Rita Hayworth treated soldiers to USO shows here. The early California missions of the region inspired the amphitheater's design.

Before Frank Sinatra, and long before Elvis, there was Rudy Valle and his megaphone. Rudy joined the Navy at the beginning of World War I, but was sent home when they found out that he was only 15. During World War II he toured with an orchestra as a member of the U.S. Coast Guard.

Rudy Valle is pictured here directing the orchestra during the dedication ceremonies of the camp's amphitheater in 1941.

Her peaches-and-cream complexion and natural acting ability earned Janet Leigh a number of high-profile roles in the late 1940s and early 1950s. Married to film star Tony Curtis and the mother of actress Jamie Lee Curtis, Janet Leigh was a favorite actress among the troops during the Korean conflict, for her role in *Psycho*.

A frequent visitor to Camp San Luis Obispo, Bob Hope is probably best known as a comedian and the guy who was always ready to fly off to entertain the troops.

One of Hollywood's most voluptuous film stars, Jane Russell is the actress made famous by Howard Hughes in the film *The Outlaw*. While mild and innocuous in today's terms, her 38-inch bust-line and low-cut cleavage was a subject of much controversy in the 1940s. Bob Hope once introduced her as "the two and only Miss Russell."

Nearly everyone knows Judy Garland as Dorothy in the classic cinema masterpiece The *Wizard of Oz*. At one of the USO shows at Camp San Luis Obispo, a young Judy Garland attempted to sing a favorite from that movie, "Over the Rainbow," while comedian Bob Hope interjected his own interpretation of the Wizard.

Harpo Marx was the second oldest of the famous Marx Brothers, and the one who never spoke on film or stage. Harpo got his name from the instrument he played and got his "taxi horn" from a 1920 Ford. Appearing in over 20 movies, he was a favorite among the troops at Camp San Luis Obispo.

One of the most popular comedy teams ever, the Three Stooges could easily lift the spirits of any troop. Their unique poking, gouging, and slap-happy antics could make any soldier laugh.

Always the joker, Bob Hope appears here with another one of his co-stars Dorothy Lamour. Dorothy was a favorite pinup girl of the troops in World War II. Her sarong-draped charms were adored by many fans, especially when she appeared in those "road" pictures with Bing Crosby and Bob Hope in which Crosby always got the girl.

Bing Crosby's brother Bob was another of the troop's favorite visitors to Camp San Luis Obispo. Bob's greatest claim to fame, besides being Bing's younger brother, was the Dixieland band that bore his name, Bob Crosby's Bob Cats. Considered one of the greatest jazz bands of all time, the visit of the Bob Crosby Orchestra was one of Camp San Luis Obispo's most memorable shows.

Interviewing a soldier as part of the USO Star Spangled Network, NBC provided a portable recording studio where a soldier could record a message and send it back home.

Six

A PERIOD OF

TRANSFORMATION

Camp San Luis Obispo once again reverted to state control in July 1956 and was again operated by the California National Guard. Responding to the need for junior officers in the California National Guard, Maj. Gen. Curtis D. O'Sullivan, adjutant general, established an officer's school for the National Guard, separate from the U.S. Army's school at Fort Benning, Georgia. The U.S. Army provided the program of instruction, ensuring that the training met the same standards as those at Fort Benning. California's Officer Candidate School (OCS) graduated its first class in 1961. That same year the Army leased Camp San Luis Obispo from the California Military Department. OCS training officially came under the newly created California Military Academy (CMA), based at the camp.

In July 1965, the camp reverted back to the State of California with operational control again under the California National Guard. Training at the camp for guardsmen during this period was conducted mostly in classrooms, although squads and platoons were sent into the field for tactical exercises. For the most part the camp's ranges and field training areas were used exclusively by the CMA. When the Watts riots erupted in August 1965 and were followed by civil disturbances in other intercity areas, and then protests against the Vietnam War on college campuses grew violent, the National Guard was forced to shift the focus of its training from conventional warfare to rapid deployment and riot control.

Throughout the tumultuous Vietnam era, the California Military Academy continued to grow and evolve. In 1974 the first women graduated from OCS and were commissioned in the National Guard. By that time college credits were earned for completion of OCS, reflecting continued accreditation by the infantry school at Fort Benning, Georgia. Since its establishment, California's Officer Candidate School has graduated more than 5,000 soldiers. In August 1979, in conjunction with OCS, a formal education program in leadership for non-commissioned officers (NCOs) at the E6 and E7 grades were conducted for the first time. Organized as the NCO Education System (NCOES) in 1981, NCO leadership training became a staple at the California Military Academy and remains so today. The 223rd Infantry Regiment continues to operate these and several other military occupational skills training programs.

The kind of training offered at officer candidate school, or OCS, can't be bought. It must be earned. It takes hard work, commitment, and drive. But when all is said and done, the soldier has an education that's worth its weight in gold.

The OCS program is designed to qualify military personnel for appointment as federally recognized second lieutenants—individuals with the required professional knowledge, character, motivation, and capabilities for leadership to function as officers in the California Army National Guard.

Inspections are routine and often times unannounced. OCS uses the same program of instruction and evaluation requirements dictated by the United States Army Infantry School, Fort Benning, Georgia.

Applicants accepted for OCS are attached to the 223rd Infantry Regiment (Combat Arms) and put through a rigid course of instruction. The OCS program is divided into segments. The student first goes through OCS orientation/in processing, and then it's onto Phase I Preparation. The third segment is OCS Phase I Annual Training at Fort Meade in June, which is followed by OCS Phase II Preparation conducted at Camp San Luis Obispo between July and September. The final segment is OCS Phase III Annual Training at Fort Lewis, Washington in August.

Pictured here is the staff of the 1972 California Military Academy. Today, these programs are conducted by the 223rd Infantry Regiment (Combat Arms), which has been designated the California Army National Guard's premier training school house for military personnel.

Here at Camp San Luis Obispo, classroom and field training is conducted according to highly professional standards and using the latest programs of instruction and high-tech automation and equipment, all to present the student with as positive a learning experience as can be obtained within the Army school system.

Ensuring that the instructors continue to be the best that the California Army National Guard has to offer, Maj. Gen. Robert C. Thrasher, adjutant general (February 1987–October 1992), inspects the troops during a tour. Members of the 223rd Infantry Regiment take great pride in presenting first-class instruction to the many student visitors that attend both from within and outside of California.

The headquarters of the 223rd Infantry Regiment (formerly the California Military Academy) is pictured here.

A longtime supporter of the California National Guard, actor Tom Selleck is just one of the California Military Academy's alumni.

Seven

INFRASTRUCTURE
AND REVITALIZATION

During the World War II and Korean War eras, Camp San Luis Obispo was like any other U.S. Army facility with very few amenities. Over the years very little funding has been provided to keep these facilities of Camp San Luis Obispo up to date. Although the 1980s and 1990s brought increased funds for the department of defense, very little trickled down to sustain base operations at Camp San Luis Obispo. The camp was considered by the U.S. Army as a local training area for transient troops during the summer.

Although Camp San Luis Obispo is a state-owned and -operated training center, the state general fund contributed less than 15 percent of the total operating budget. Since the end of the Korean War, the camp has managed to exist and operate within its very conservative budget.

Lacking the necessary funding to transform Camp San Luis Obispo into a modern military post, a plan was developed to systematically refurbish many of the outdated World War II–era buildings. Buildings were first inspected and those that were found to be structurally sound were identified for preservation. The remaining buildings were systematically demolished. With its small full-time staff, some inmate labor from the neighboring California Men's Colony, and the dedication and commitment of the guardsmen, the existing buildings are being transformed into modern state-of-the-art classrooms at a fraction of the cost of building new ones.

While infrastructure revitalization and rehabilitation of its training facilities have increased at Camp San Luis Obispo, costs for this construction have been kept extremely low. Over the course of the last ten years Camp San Luis Obispo has undergone a complete transformation while still operating within its conservative budget constraints.

Like other federal and state training facilities in California, Camp San Luis Obispo continues to evolve. Today, Camp San Luis Obispo is in the process of an ongoing transformation that will make it into one of the National Guard's finest state-of-the-art classroom and field training centers in the nation.

To ensure the continued availability of training lands and facilities in support of the California National Guard, through responsible environmental stewardship and compliance with all applicable environmental laws and regulations, Camp San Luis Obispo is in a constant process of infrastructure revitalization. Today, buildings that once served as old 1940s- and 1950s-era company mess halls are being converted into state-of-the-art classrooms.

Training can take place in many ways. Camp San Luis Obispo's primary mission is to develop and maintain both land and air facilities; to support the administration, training, and readiness of the California Army and Air National Guard; and to develop and enhance relationships to maximize the value of the facilities to the soldiers and the communities they serve.

Bringing these buildings up to today's building and usage standards is no easy task; however, the project give National Guard construction units and engineers a place to hone their skills while contributing to the modernization process here at Camp San Luis Obispo. Here a guardsman installs new electrical outlets and T-1 communication cables.

Today's training missions differ greatly from the 1940s and 1950s. So it is understandable that the process of infrastructure revitalization would include repairing roofs and adding new roofing tiles. The addition of insulation and fire sprinkler systems in the attic areas and new electrical and plumbing would also be incorporated. Pictured here is framing for restrooms and offices being added.

Revitalization also includes the process of ensuring every aspect of construction meets current building codes. In this picture, guardsmen install new plumbing for the restrooms.

Old plumbing dating back to the 1940s is rapidly being replaced. Systematically new water, sewer, and electrical lines are replacing the existing infrastructure at Camp San Luis Obispo. Here a guardsman prepares to install new plastic plumbing.

Camp San Luis Obispo also believes that environmental stewardship includes drastically reducing energy consumption on the post. Insulation is being added and walls and ceilings are being covered with drywall.

With the drywall work completed and air conditioning ducts now added, these guardsmen begin the work of preparing the building for painting.

With new insulation and state-of-the-art fire sprinkler systems installed, these guardsmen apply the finishing touches to the drywall.

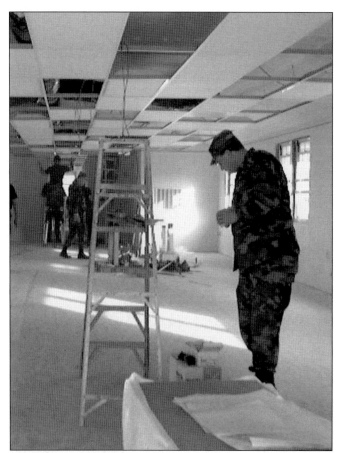

With the building now painted, guardsmen begin the process of installing new lighting fixtures and drop ceilings.

To further reduce energy consumption, old windows are replaced with new double-pane windows and some openings are covered. Pictured here are the final preparations being made to the outside of the building before guardsmen begin the process of wrapping the building.

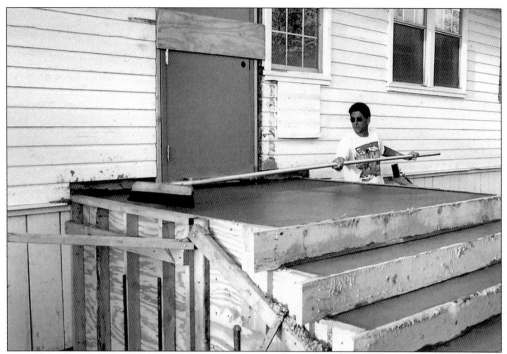

Post engineers pour concrete entryways, replacing the old wooden steps that once stood in their place. New steel doors replace wooden doors. After damaged areas are repaired, the building is wrapped and, finally, stucco and a color coating are added.

With the outside of the building now stuccoed with a color coating, the final cosmetic touches, such as trim, are added to the outside of the structure. Here guardsmen install the new air conditioning units.

After a transformation, these buildings have become state-of-the-art classrooms while also having served as training areas for engineering and construction units.

Working with the federal government, the California Military Department is making every effort to continue this revitalization process to ensure that Camp San Luis Obispo will continue to be one of the nation's largest and most versatile state-owned training facilities.

Eight
CAMP SAN LUIS OBISPO TODAY

Camp San Luis Obispo is still one of the nation's largest and most versatile state-owned training areas. During the last decade, several federal training facilities in California have been closed or have had their operations greatly reduced. Ironically, Camp San Luis Obispo continues to be a vital training center for both the U.S. Army and California National Guard. Its ideal location on California's Central Coast and the quality of its field and garrison facilities continue to make Camp San Luis Obispo one of the most useful, versatile, and productive training installations in the country.

Even though Camp San Luis Obispo is a state-owned and -operated training facility, much of the funding needed to sustain operations comes from the federal government as part of a cooperative agreement for training National Guard troops in a federal status. Facility administration has been kept to a minimum with 29 full-time post headquarters personnel and a staff of 782 civilian and military personnel. These dedicated men and women support the approximately 343,000 personnel representing military, civilian, and law enforcement agencies that use Camp San Luis Obispo yearly for classroom and field training operations, as well as the camp's 24 permanent tenants.

The camp continues to support the training missions of several federal and state agencies as well as providing classroom, field, and infantry tactical training for the National Guard. The camp also maintains ample supporting facilities, including a chapel, two service clubs, a 750-seat theater, a laundromat, tailoring services, a barbershop, an exchange, and a heliport (O'Sullivan Army Heliport) that can accommodate military rotary wing aircraft.

Whether it is in support of our peace-time training mission, war-time training mission, homeland security, riot suppression, counter–drug trafficking, or disaster preparedness and response, Camp San Luis Obispo continues to serve as a primary staging area for this state and offers the training facilities required by government and civilian agencies at the local, state and federal levels.

Camp San Luis Obispo has persevered through the Great Depression, World War II, the Korean War, the Vietnam War, the Gulf War, the Iraq War, dramatic social change, natural disasters, and riots and has served the people of California and this nation faithfully. Now, more than 75 years since its founding, Camp San Luis Obispo remains undiminished, living up to its motto: "Support with Excellence!"

Following the federal government's closure of Fort Irwin and Camp Roberts as National Guard training facilities in the 1970s, the California Army National Guard once again returned to its original home at Camp San Luis Obispo. Ironically, with the transfer of Camp Roberts to the control of the California Army National Guard, Camp San Luis Obispo has remained the state's primary training facility for specialized training of the National Guard.

The present-day headquarters building is the operations center for all of Camp San Luis Obispo.

Camp San Luis Obispo is also the home to the 223rd Infantry (Combat Arms) Regiment. This unit is responsible for the instruction of California's Officer Candidate School (OCS) established by the California Military Academy during the 1960s and the NCO School House launched in the 1980s.

The headquarters for the 223rd Infantry (Combat Arms) Regiment is located in the camp's old headquarters building. Built during World War II, this building served as the post's headquarters throughout the Korea and Vietnam eras.

Camp San Luis Obispo's classrooms come in various sizes to meet the training needs of those agencies utilizing the facility. Through its revitalization program, Camp San Luis Obispo continues to foster economic development, improved educational levels, and information access for the National Guard as well as non–department of defense activities (other federal government agencies, state/local governments, and organizations and individuals).

In support of both federal and state missions, these revitalized classrooms aid the California National Guard's readiness by providing increased access to military training and education facilities.

Smaller mess hall facilities have been added to support smaller commands utilizing Camp San Luis Obispo during training.

In order to meet the National Guard's training needs, even the 1941-built PerLee Theater recently underwent a renovation of its own. Originally known as the War Department Theater, it was later renamed PerLee Theater after California's first adjutant general, Brig. Gen. Theron R. PerLee.

Pictured here is one of the six 160-person barracks that have been constructed to meet the housing needs of the multiple training units that utilize the facilities here at Camp San Luis Obispo.

In addition to Camp San Luis Obispo's six 160-person barracks, several older barracks, many of which were built in the 1940s, have been renovated to provide additional barrack facilities for smaller commands training on the facility.

Camp San Luis Obispo continues to be home to the United States Property and Fiscal Office (USPFO), which provides fiscal support to the State of California and is the responsible authority for paying active-duty soldiers of the California National Guard, as well as for the procurement, distribution, tracking, and accounting of all federal property and funds allocated by the National Guard Bureau for the State of California.

These supply buildings were constructed in the early 1940s and continue to provide the State of California with logistical supply support for National Guard troops training at Camp San Luis Obispo.

The National Guard Bureau initially established the National Interagency Civil-Military Institute (NICI) in 1989 to train military personnel and civilian agencies in the war against drugs. In the late 1990s, while maintaining its emphasis on inter-agency training, NICI began to expand its counter drug training to other areas of Military Support to Civil Authorities (MSCA), including anti-terrorism and force protection curricula.

Whether on topics of homeland security, crowd control, counter drug, disaster preparedness, or consequence management, Camp San Luis Obispo continues to offer classroom training specific to government and civilian agencies at the local, county, state, and federal levels.

Technology is changing the way guardsman train, educate, and operate in the California National Guard. Classrooms are also utilized as distributed (distance) learning centers. Distributed learning is simply another effective method of training.

Although distributed learning will not replace resident training, the California National Guard is conducting more training using distance education and, in some cases, providing troops with an alternative to traditional resident training. In other cases, these centers serve to augment resident training or replace resident training altogether. Through distance learning centers, higher levels of readiness can be achieved and sustained.

Camp San Luis Obispo also operates a Military Operations in Urban Training (MOUT) village of more than 60 acres and consisting of residential, commercial, and industrial replicated structures. The village is designed to support multi-echelon training scenarios, and also features a vehicle pursuit course designed to support both military and civilian training exercises in the training of drivers, convoy and check point operations, law enforcement, etc.

To enhance the California National Guard's readiness and mobilization levels, Camp San Luis Obispo is in the process of upgrading its existing M4 and M16 range and M9 combat pistol qualification range to meet the future training and development criteria.

The California Specialized Training Institute (CSTI) was established by the Office of Emergency Services (OES) as a center to assist in the training and cross-training of military, law enforcement, fire departments, and other disaster and public emergency agencies.

California's success in meeting the challenges of this state's emergencies and disasters can be directly attributed to an emergency management and response system that has been developed and taught at Camp San Luis Obispo by such training agencies as the California Specialized Training Institute and National Interagency Civil-Military Institute.

The California National Guard has been involved in providing support to California's youth since 1911, when the Military and Veterans Code authorized the formation of the California Cadet Corps. Since that time California National Guard men and women have been involved in numerous youth-oriented programs such as the Civil Air Patrol at Camp San Luis Obispo.

Pictured here are members of the Sea Cadets. Camp San Luis Obispo has been a longtime home to the Sea Cadets, a non-profit civilian education organization federally incorporated in 1962 to educate youth about the role of the maritime services in national defense and in maintaining the economic viability of our nation.

Congress enacted legislation in the 1990s authorizing the National Guard, as part of its domestic mission, to conduct the ChalleNGe program. The mission of the Grizzly Youth Academy is to intervene in the life of an at-risk teenager and produce a program graduate with the values, skills, education, and self-discipline necessary to succeed as an adult.

The California National Guard established the Grizzly Youth Academy at Camp San Luis Obispo in 1998. The ChalleNGe program consists of three phases; a 2-week pre-ChalleNGe phase, a 20-week residential ChalleNGe phase, and a 12-month post-residential phase. Here students are pictured during the pre-ChalleNGe phase of training where they are taught the basics of physical fitness, health, and self-discipline.

Angel Gate Academy is a four-week residential program offered to students of the Los Angeles Unified School District (LAUSD) and conducted at Camp San Luis Obispo. This is a learning and intervention program for sixth- to eighth-grade boys and girls, ages 11 to 13, and considered "at-risk." Students follow an intense academic course of instruction, work in computer labs, and participate in life science field trips.

Members from the National Guard teach and instill self-discipline, citizenship, self-respect, leadership, and teamwork. Evaluation of the program indicates that dropout rates have been reduced by 72 percent, reading scores improved by an average of two grade levels, and disciplinary action significantly decreased. Additionally, parents of students attending Angel Gate Academy receive parenting education that has proven to enhance the learning environment at home.

113

Camp San Luis Obispo is also home to the California Conservation Corps and the California Conservation Corps State Museum. Patterned after the Civilian Conservation Corps of the 1930s and 1940s, the California Conservation Corps was launched by Gov. Jerry Brown in 1973. The California Conservation Corps continues to play a vital role in the preservation of California's resources.

Stepping back in time, the California Conservation Corps State Museum documents both the youth corps movement of the 20th century and the history of the Civilian Conservation Corps in California. Complete with tools, uniforms, and other artifacts used by Roosevelt's "Forest Army," the museum has over 100 binders containing photos of "CCC boys" in camps, documentation of camp locations and the work done, letters written home, discharge papers, and much more.

Nine

MUSEUM AND HISTORICAL PRESERVATION

As Camp San Luis Obispo continues to undergo infrastructure revitalization and rehabilitation of its training facilities, key elements of a rich military history may be lost. This presents both the California Army National Guard and the State of California with the interesting and significant challenge of preserving the camp's history while continuing to improve the facility's ability to support and sustain a modern military mission.

As a historic site, Camp San Luis Obispo has a unique opportunity to create and preserve a piece of California's military heritage. The California Center for Military History is working with Camp San Luis Obispo in the development of an "in house" historical preservation plan that provides for refurbishing structures of historical significance and recording important camp events and the achievements of the officers and troops who called the post "home." Camp San Luis Obispo has recently published a historical driving tour guide, which not only provides a map of the camp but also information on the camp buildings and training areas. The next phase of the historical preservation program will include using one of the camp's existing structures for the display of artifacts. The camp will also erect display cases in several of the camp classrooms as a means of educating troops and visitors. Another phase envisions relocating the current display of Army aviation assets to the O'Sullivan Army Airfield at the west end of the camp.

The final and most exciting phase of the program calls for the modification of one of the camp's historical structures into a state-of-the-art conference facility that would include a dedicated museum and library wing. This museum would display the many items of historical interest currently lost to the public, allowing students, laymen, and historians alike to have a place to study the rich history of Camp San Luis Obispo. To help preserve and protect the legacy of our soldiers and airmen who have trained at Camp San Luis Obispo, the establishment of this museum has become a joint effort of the California State Military Museum in Sacramento and the California Center for Military History. For further information, you may write to

California Center for Military History
Camp San Luis Obispo Museum Annex
Post Office Box 4360
San Luis Obispo, California 93403-4360

A relic of an earlier era, this gate was moved from its original location off old Highway 1 to its present location by the camp's engineers and the Operating Engineers Trust in 1986.

Today, the main entrance onto Camp San Luis Obispo is through the original main gate of the

The present guardhouse was constructed at the approximate location of the sentry post used during World War II when the U.S. Army erected the new camp headquarters on this side of Highway 1.

National Guard Training Camp that was placed on the grounds in 1928.

Restored to its original splendor, the gate was moved to its present location in 1986, by

This photograph shows the original historical marker of 1928.

engineers who were careful to incorporate the unique historic markers.

ORIGINAL GATES
OF
CAMP SAN LUIS OBISPO

ORIGINAL HOME OF THE CALIFORNIA
NATIONAL GUARD

CONSTRUCTED 1928
RELOCATED 1986

TOTAL WEIGHT 100 TONS
INAUGURAL SITE THREE QUARTERS OF A MILE EAST

DEDICATED TO ALL NATIONAL GUARD SOLDIERS
PAST, PRESENT AND FUTURE

This historic marker tells the history of these rock gates.

The original headquarters of the National Guard Training Camp, built in 1928, appears very much the same as it did at that time. This building served also as Camp Merriam's headquarters until 1941 when Camp Merriam was turned over to the U.S. Army. The old headquarters building is scheduled to be restored, complete with its old mess hall at the rear of the building that still contains the old stove and ice box used to serve officers as early as 1929.

Just past the original headquarters building were two regimental areas established on the plateau east of the parade ground. Located southeast of the parade ground are a couple of the mess halls of the original camp that still remain today. The wooden window protectors served two purposes: securing the buildings when not in use and, when folded down, doubling as instant tables on which to serve meals.

Located on the grass meridian at the camp's entrance is the Italian "Prisoner of War" rock, a concrete monument made by Salvatore Fossati, an Italian prisoner of war in 1944. American forces captured Fossati along with 250,000 other Italian and German soldiers in Tunisia, North Africa in May 1943. Fossati was with one of two Italian prisoner of war companies to spend the war at Camp San Luis Obispo.

Southwest Signal School plaque signifies that in December of 1951 the Southwestern Signal Corps Training Center (SWSS) was established at Camp San Luis Obispo. The SWSS became the third Signal Corps Center in operation, joining others at Fort Monmouth, New Jersey and Camp Gordon, Georgia.

The California National Guard "For Country and Humanity" statue, created by artist Haig Patigan, stands some seven feet in height above a four-foot-high base. Cast in waterproof light grey cement, this four-figured statue was exhibited in the State Building at the 1939 World's Fair on Treasure Island in the San Francisco Bay.. The statue was removed to Camp Merriam (Camp San Luis Obispo) on the suggestion of Maj. Gen. Walter P. Story, then commanding general of the 40th Division. It features a guardsman and an armored woman bearing a sword and flag, each representing "Patriotism." Completing the statue are two other feminine figures, an adult in the rear and an adolescent in the fore, representing "Humanity."

Pictured here is the grass meridian, or main mall, of Camp San Luis Obispo where several static displays of historic significance may be viewed. On the hill opposite the main gate is the camp's OCS eagle, placed there in the early 1970s by cadets attending the California Military Academy.

This airplane is the first F-4C Phantom II Fighter-Bomber that the 163rd Tactical Fighter Group at March AFB received when it converted from the O-2A aircraft. Brigadier General (then Captain) Lucas and Major General (then Major) Gibson delivered this plane to March Air Force Base in October 1982. When the unit converted to the more modern F-4E in 1987, this particular F-4C was flown to Mather Air Force Base and put on static display. In 1996, after Mather Air Force Base was closed, the airplane was disassembled and trucked on flatbeds to Camp San Luis Obispo, where it was reassembled. The names of pilots Lucas and Gibson are still inscribed on the canopy rails.

This two-man–crewed machine-gun tank is one of only two World War II–vintage Japanese-type 97B tankettes that can be found in the U.S. military's historical inventory today.

Representative of several historical military aircraft on display at Camp San Luis Obispo is the CH-47A Chinook helicopter manufactured by Boeing Vertol and pictured here. Other such vintage aircraft include the CH-34 Choctaw, OH-23 Raven, H-19 Chickasaw, and H-13 Sioux helicopters, and several airplanes including the O-1 Birddog or U-6 Beaver. The camp also has the Nike-Hercules surface-to-air missile and the Sergeant surface-to-surface missile on display, as well as a 1939 Seagrave fire engine.

The Bataan Memorial, also located on the grass meridian, has been dedicated to commemorate the Battle of Luzon at Lamon Bay, Philippine Islands on December 26, 1941. The 2nd Platoon, Company C, 194th Tank Battalion from Salinas, California, commanded by Staff Sgt. Emil C. Morello, came face to face with an enemy roadblock. Without any hesitation, the tank smashed into the roadblock and the Japanese gun behind it. Before being hit, Morello's tank fired on other gun positions. Morello and his crew escaped the next morning only to be either killed or captured, along with the other members of the 192nd and 194th Tank Battalions at Bataan.

The 15 remaining veterans of Company C officially dedicated the Bataan Memorial in 1998. This memorial displays the heroism and gallantry of Company C, 194th Tank Battalion, formally the 40th Tank Company, and members of the American and Filipino Army regiments who were either killed or captured in that struggle that included the Bataan Death March. The 192nd and 194th Tank Battalions were National Guard units and were both awarded three Presidential Unit Citations for their gallantry in action. Today's 1st Battalion, 149th Armor, California Army National Guard carries on the gallant traditions of the 194th Tank Battalion.

The uniforms and photographs pictured in the background show the humble beginnings of Camp San Luis Obispo's museum. Camp San Luis Obispo is working closely with the California State Military Museum in Sacramento and the California Center for Military History to establish a state-of-the-art museum complex to preserve the military history of Camp San Luis Obispo.

California State Military Museum

The California State Military Museum is a part of the United States Army Museum System and is the official military and historical research center for the State of California. Located just blocks from the State Capitol, in the Old Sacramento Historical Park, the museum is operated for the California State Military Department by the California Military Museum Foundation, an IRS 501(c)(3) non-profit educational organization, and is supported by the California Center for Military History (CCMH). A major command of the California State Military Reserve (CA SMR), the CCMH provides support to the California National Guard's historical, command information, recruiting, and community relations programs, and provides augmentation services for the California State Military Museum as an affiliate activity of the U.S. Army Center of Military History.

The Maj. Gen. Walter P. Story Library and Resource Center, located in the basement of the California State Military Museum in Sacramento, has one of the finest collections of military histories in the western United States. With over 10,000 volumes and growing rapidly, the library is one of the state's educational and historical treasures. The California State Military Museum also operates four satellite museums: Camp Roberts Museum Annex, Camp San Luis Obispo Historical Site, the 40th Infantry Division Museum at the Joint Forces Training Center (Los Alamitos), and the 185th Armor and 251st Coast Artillery Regimental Museum (San Diego).

The California State Military Museum works to improve public awareness of the importance of California's military contributions to the community, state, and nation. It proudly serves the general public, students, historians, and members of the armed forces in the preservation of this segment of history for present and future generations. For further information, you may write to

California State Military Museum
1119 Second Street
Sacramento, California 95814

or

California Center for Military History
Post Office Box 661588
Sacramento, California 95866-1588

or visit us on the web at www.militarymuseum.org